IMAGES
of America

THE SWISS COLONY

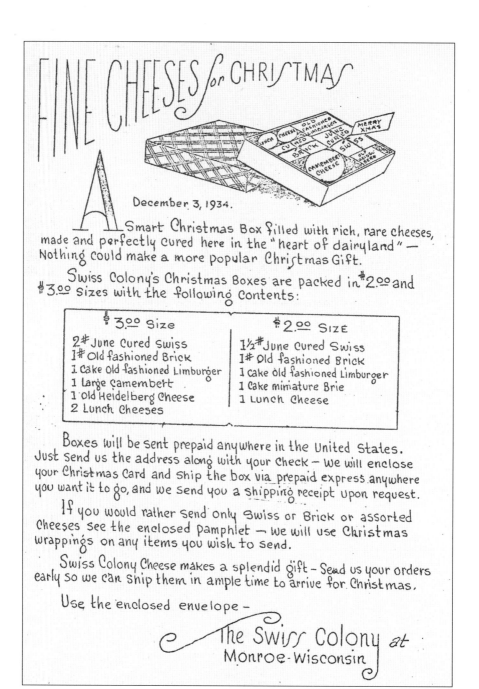

FINE CHEESES for CHRISTMAS

December 3, 1934.

A Smart Christmas Box filled with rich, rare cheeses, made and perfectly cured here in the "heart of dairyland" — Nothing could make a more popular Christmas Gift.

Swiss Colony's Christmas Boxes are packed in $2.00 and $3.00 Sizes with the following Contents:

$3.00 Size	$2.00 Size
2# June Cured Swiss	1½# June Cured Swiss
1# Old fashioned Brick	1# Old fashioned Brick
1 Cake Old fashioned Limburger	1 Cake Old fashioned Limburger
1 Large Camembert	1 Cake miniature Brie
1 Old Heidelberg Cheese	1 Lunch Cheese
2 Lunch Cheeses	

Boxes will be sent prepaid anywhere in the United States. Just send us the address along with your check — we will enclose your Christmas Card and ship the box via prepaid express anywhere you want it to go, and we send you a shipping receipt upon request.

If you would rather send only Swiss or Brick or assorted Cheeses see the enclosed pamphlet — we will use Christmas wrappings on any items you wish to send.

Swiss Colony Cheese makes a splendid gift — Send us your orders early so we can ship them in ample time to arrive for Christmas.

Use the enclosed envelope —

The Swiss Colony at Monroe · Wisconsin

EARLY SELLING. One of the first pieces The Swiss Colony used was this mimeographed, one-page flyer that was in use eight years after the company was founded. Seven nice cuts of cheese were being sold for $3, including shipping cost, to anywhere in the United States. The first year, 1926, Raymond R. (Ray) Kubly shipped a total of 50 packages. By 1938, between 6,000 and 7,000 were shipped.

On the cover: **PROCESSING CHEESE.** A group of Swiss Colony associates package Swiss cheese in the 1940s. They are using a special new foil (for that era) to securely wrap the cuts of delectable cheese.

IMAGES
of America

THE SWISS COLONY

Jim Glessner

ARCADIA

Published by Arcadia Publishing
Charleston SC, Chicago IL, Portsmouth NH, San Francisco CA

Printed in the United States of America

Library of Congress Catalog Card Number: 2006920996

For all general information contact Arcadia Publishing at:
Telephone 843-853-2070
Fax 843-853-0044
E-mail sales@arcadiapublishing.com
For customer service and orders:
Toll-Free 1-888-313-2665

Visit us on the internet at http://www.arcadiapublishing.com

MAGNIFICENT COURTHOUSE. This is the downtown square of Monroe, home of The Swiss Colony. The Green County Courthouse, built in 1891, still anchors the downtown area. The cornerstone laying ceremony on August 27 of that year drew two state supreme court justices and about 5,000 county residents. This early photograph shows horses and buggies around the courthouse.

CONTENTS

ACKNOWLEDGMENTS

The following folks were extremely helpful in assisting with photographs and background information for this book: Sheila Berrey and Deb Weis, Public Relations Department; Marge Edler, administrative assistant to Forrest L. Kubly and archivist; Jan Burgener and the Photo Studio staff; and Deb Davis, administrative assistant. Thanks to all of The Swiss Colony.

To my wife, Lois, kids, and grandkids, much love for letting me pursue a dream to document the impressive Swiss Colony story.

GROWING PAINS. From early beginnings of operations by Ray Kubly in the basement of the Kubly family residence, the fledgling company moved into a succession of buildings before expanding to Monroe's Cheese Row. The company occupied the space immediately to the left of the Kraft Foods building on the right. Cheese Row was located south of the square shown on page 4.

INTRODUCTION

A true rags-to-riches story encompasses The Swiss Colony, headquartered in Monroe in a pastoral setting with hills and dales, farms, cows, and cheese.

The company's founding was most unique. Founder Ray Kubly was a senior at the University of Wisconsin, Madison, when he and two fellow students drew up an advertising campaign for a marketing class project. It seems a professor had mentioned that someone ought to be selling cheese by mail.

The seeds for the company's beginning were sown. Kubly, in 1926, mimeographed and stamped handbills that offered cuts of bulk cheese, which he mailed to anyone he thought might respond. By enlisting the aid of a local Railway Express agent, who contacted fellow agents for names of customers who might be interested in good cheese, potential customers were secured. As orders came trickling in, he descended into the family basement to cut the huge wheels by butcher knife into pieces that he wrapped and packaged for shipment. That first year, all of 50 packages were sold.

Fifty packages were not sufficient to keep bread on the table, and Kubly would hold down "day jobs" for the next 35 years. When he was vice president and general manager of Lakeshire-Marty (a division of the Borden Company) in 1961, he finally turned his attention to his own company.

Following the Depression era and struggling times, the company began to grow and, by 1938, outgrew the Kubly house. Space was rented in a variety of local buildings. By 1941, Christmas employment had grown to 100 and a payroll of $19,000.

By 1948, a new mail-handling record was established in Monroe, when unprecedented demand for packages of cheese required the Milwaukee Road to provide an extra boxcar daily from December 9 until the Christmas holiday for the exclusive loading of parcel post items. In 1950, cancellations at the Monroe Post Office hit a peak of 48,900 on a single day, attributable to the increase in Christmas gift packages mailed by the firm. In 1954, The Swiss Colony was incorporated.

Sadly, on February 16, 1968, Ray Kubly succumbed to a heart attack. One of his sons, Raymond R. Kubly Jr. (known as Pat), who had been named president just the year before, inherited the company reins. He guided the steady growth in the next decades, with constant innovations and new and fresh marketing ideas.

In 1979, the company began diversifying into nonfood catalogs with the introduction of the Gift Collection. This evolved into the Seventh Avenue catalog, which eventually became an affiliated company in 1986. Other product and theme-specific catalogs followed. Today the "stable" of marketing venues includes two food catalogs and five general merchandise catalogs, all of which are now affiliated companies. These affiliates are: Seventh Avenue, Inc., The Tender Filet, Inc., Ginny's, Inc., Midnight Velvet, Inc., Through the Country Door, Inc., and Monroe & Main, Inc.

Internet retailing and infomercials are also extensively used. The Swiss Colony also created a data center and a marketing company to help support the catalog business and outside clients.

Today The Swiss Colony and its affiliates are located in 12 different Midwestern communities. There are about 1,200 regular employees and almost 6,000 temporary employees. They operate from 1.8 million square feet of owned and leased buildings. In 2004, the companies shipped almost 12 million gift packs from its various locations.

To efficiently deliver merchandise to its customers, The Swiss Colony has delved into cutting-edge technology, plus data-based marketing and credit applications. The heavy investment of both capital and personnel has allowed The Swiss Colony to become one of the larger direct marketers in the United States.

And it all started with selling cheese!

TONS OF CHEESE. Other types of cheese were also marketed in the early days. Here a young Kurt Schwager (left) discusses the merits of a cut of cheese, presumably cheddar, with two unidentified gentlemen. They are standing amid immense stacks of cheese in The Swiss Colony's original cheese cellar on Cheese Row during the mid-1950s.

One

IN THE BEGINNING, IT WAS CHEESE

For a midnight snack last night, had some Swiss cheese from
Wisconsin (from The Swiss Colony) and it was better
than the Swiss cheese I had in Switzerland.
—E. V. Darling, columnist for the
Los Angeles Examiner, January 16, 1940

EARLY CHEESE FACTORY. The abundance of cheese factories in the rolling hills of Green County inspired Ray Kubly to offer cuts of Swiss cheese to the multitudes via mail. This photograph, taken at the Foley Factory in 1935, features little Bob Kessler (in front), who spent his adult life as a cheese grader for The Swiss Colony. An early cheese maker, unidentified, is at right. Farms in the county in 1949 had the highest "gross farm income per farm" of any county in Wisconsin, because of cheese.

WHERE IT STARTED. The house where company founder Ray Kubly first started cutting cheese is still standing in Monroe. Here young Kubly used a butcher knife to "chunk" cheese into smaller pieces for mail-order sales.

CHEESE ROW. A sketch by Beau Payton, entitled "Cheese Row at Christmastime," pictures an early company home. This view is from the opposite angle of the one on page 6. The Swiss Colony building was the second one from the end (to the left of the pole). The Milwaukee Road Rail

Depot is shown to the right. The historic depot was salvaged in 1993 and moved to a new location and now serves as the county welcome center and home to the Historic Cheesemaking Center.

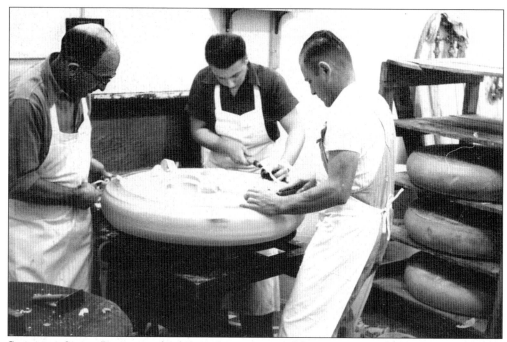

SCRAPING SWISS. Preparing wheel Swiss for cutting was labor intensive. Here associates, from left to right, Al Waelti, Al Hixson, and Werner Adler scrape the rind from a wheel. This was done to get at the "heart" of the cheese, which was then cut into chunks and wrapped for shipment.

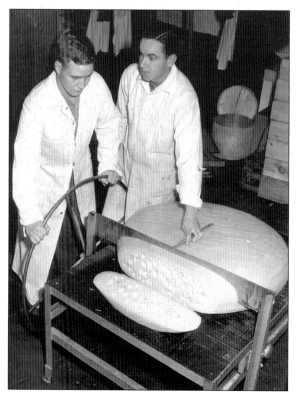

REAL CUTUPS. After the cheese was scraped, it then was pieced. From left to right, Bob Hardel and Raymond Rupnow use a hand-powered cutter to work the huge wheels into smaller "cuts." This photograph is from 1946.

QUALITY CHEESE. Bob Kessler, known as Kessie to his coworkers, became a symbol of The Swiss Colony's quest for excellence. In these two photographs, Kessler conducts a "plugging" operation, where a sample of cheese is removed from the wheel to see if it has matured enough to sell. The tool used was called a "trier." Swiss Colony cheese was reputed to be the best because Kessler, a cheese grader, saw to it that it was the best.

CONSUMER PORTIONS. In another operation, block chunks of cheese were cut into smaller portions and wrapped in the Cut Cheese Department. Here Dawn Wirth (left) and Stan Campbell run the line.

FOR GROCERY STORES. In the early days, The Swiss Colony also performed a slicing operation with their cheese. Here the block chunks of Swiss are cut into slices before being portioned, weighed, and packaged into consumer-size units for retail firms such as A&P food stores. This operation took place at the old Borden building in Monroe. The associates are unidentified.

A Lot of Handwork. Many hands made light work in a variety of tasks at the growing company. In the top photograph, employees dip cuts of cheese in wax to preserve them for shipping. In the bottom photograph, the waxed and wrapped pieces of cheese are sorted according to weight. These early workers are unidentified.

ASSEMBLY LINE. Pieces of cut cheese of many varieties were accumulated after the cutting and wrapping operation and then arranged into a gift pack that was both mouthwatering and visually attractive. These early associates, unidentified, use a moving conveyer belt system to assemble the gift packs.

ANOTHER PIONEERING SOLUTION. Up to 1952, all gift assortments were packed with the cheese pieces surrounded by shredded green tissue, which needed to be clipped and scissor trimmed by hand. A faster method had to be found due to growth and demand. Molded green plastic was developed that would provide a separate compartment for each piece of cheese and was the ideal solution.

CHRISTMAS BASKETS. By 1967, gift designers had perfected assembling cheese cuts and other gift components into a basket motif. Bea Goecks packed this "Fireside Basket" during that time period.

NO LEANING TOWERS ALLOWED. Gift packing further evolved in the 1970s as "tower" gifts were invented. These really difficult-to-assemble units were built by a crack unidentified crew of assemblers. These towers were popular with customers, who were delighted to open smaller gifts in an endless variety.

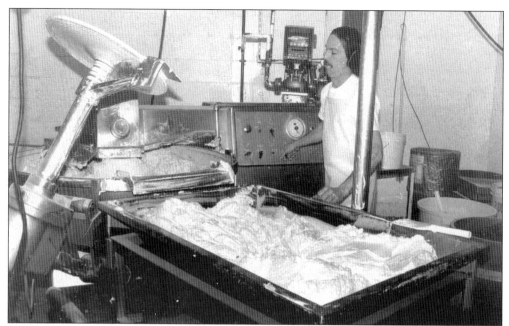

FROM CHEESE TO SPREADS. Cheese spreads became an important part of The Swiss Colony's product line in 1947, when Ray Kubly purchased Chalet Cheese Company from Karl Schwager. Chalet was renamed Enchanted Cheese and, still later, incorporated into The Swiss Colony. Schwager had initiated the "club" cheese concept in the club cars on transcontinental rail lines. The top photograph shows cheese blends being mixed by Rudy Gerber. An outgrowth of the club concept was cheese balls, flavorful mixes formed into ball shapes and then rolled in a variety of nuts or other herb blends. In the bottom photograph, an unidentified employee rolls cheese balls in nuts.

A MELEE OF ACTIVITY. Even in 1947, getting the gift packages to the customer was a daunting task. This photograph, taken on December 21, shows the Monroe Post Office processing Swiss Colony gifts.

BY RAIL, NATIONWIDE. Even earlier, in 1938, shipments were being made by Rail Express. This load of about 400 packages, in December of that year, totaled two to three tons of cheese in weight. The Rail Express employees are unidentified. Early newspaper reports indicated extra railcars were brought to Monroe to handle the volume.

OVERWHELMING. Even the postal service had trouble keeping up. This early photograph of Monroe postmaster John J. Burkhard shows him looking into a Milwaukee Road boxcar of mailbags, all containing Swiss Colony packages.

MORE SPACE NEEDED. In 1948, the volume of gifts was so large that a supplementary, temporary post office had to be secured. This view is of the Armory Building in Monroe on December 18, at the height of the Christmas rush as workers scramble to process Swiss Colony packages and get them to waiting customers. That year, about one million pounds of cheese were processed, wrapped, and assembled into gift packages.

TRUCK TRANSIT ARRIVES. As motor vehicles, trucks in particular, became more dependable, The Swiss Colony started using truck transportation in addition to relying on the railroad to ship gifts. In the foreground of this photograph, from left to right, Walter "Chink" Loertscher, Oscar Moldenhauer, and Win Haberman load gift packs into a truck.

An Alp of Catalogs. All those gifts had to start somewhere. This photograph, from the 1970s, shows a man-made mountain of catalogs that were part of more than 10 million mailed to Swiss Colony customers. These were at the R. R. Donnelley and Sons printing plant in Warsaw, Indiana. Eighty semitrailers were needed to transport them to Monroe, where they were made ready for distribution. Jim Rapp, a Donnelley representative, views the immense stack.

MORE MOUNTAINS. Once processed and labeled, the catalogs were sent to customers. Loren Elmer, supervisor of mailing in 1967, sits atop a small mountain of mailbags containing catalogs.

IT TAKES ORGANIZATION. The Monroe Fulfillment Department becomes as busy as an anthill during the annual Christmas rush, when 1,200 temporary employees join the regular Monroe staff to fill orders. This photograph shows the inspectors, who still inspect 100 percent of the outgoing shipments for accuracy. The machine at the back of the photograph shrink-wraps the various gift packs of an order into one shippable package.

IT IS NOT ALL BUSINESS, THOUGH. In the 1980s, Larry Goodman of the Fulfillment Department takes a break from the serious business of playing Santa to The Swiss Colony's customers to play Santa to his amused coworkers.

NATURE TAKES A TOLL. The Swiss Colony has had its brushes with catastrophes over the years. On Palm Sunday, April 11, 1965, a huge tornado devastated parts of Monroe, including The Swiss Colony's main packing plant. This photograph shows what was left of the parking lot at a local car dealership.

BLIZZARD. In April 1973, one of those renowned vicious Wisconsin snowstorms (blizzards) dropped about a foot of snow and buried The Swiss Colony, as evidenced by the two people trying to dig out a vehicle.

ROOF COLLAPSE. That 1973 snowstorm also was too heavy for the roof structure of the main building in Monroe. Note the cave-in of the roofing structure above one of the shipping docks.

MORE SNOW. Another traffic-stopper blasted Monroe in 1982, but that did not stop "Everybody's Santa" from doing business as usual.

NEW BUILDING. The current Swiss Colony main plant was erected in 1965–1966, and this shows the front shortly after its completion. This brought many Swiss Colony operations under one roof, but renovations continue to this day. In 2003, a major retrofit of the plant was started, with completion scheduled for 2006, bringing the facility into a more modern configuration.

SUMMER FINERY. This is how The Swiss Colony main offices look today. This photograph, taken at the height of summer flower bloom, illustrates the fine landscaping that graces the front of the building.

Two

THE OLD-WORLD PATISSERIE COMES TO AMERICA

From European "dobos," there followed petits fours and fruitcake, gingerbread and butter toffee. Today it is all these, plus truffles and brownie pockets and myriad inventions to tease the palate.

First Konditour. Karl Schwager (right), known as the father of The Swiss Colony Bakery, works with Fred Wiesinger (center), The Swiss Colony's first konditour, and a Mr. Nagy from the Zauner Pastry Shop of Bad Ischl, Austria. Wiesinger was recruited by Schwager to help form The Swiss Colony Bakery. He was followed by nine more konditours in the next few years.

Will It Ship? One of the first projects faced was to adapt the dobosh torte so it would stand up to the rigors of shipping. Wiesinger and Schwager worked on the cake layers, which were changed from a brittle product to a moister, more durable layer, thus enabling mail shipment.

FIRST LOCATION. The first bakery site was located in this building in downtown Monroe in 1959. The front of the building was used as the first Swiss Colony retail store, with the bakery in the rear. Today the site is used as the Studio 906 hair salon, and the building has not changed much since its first usage.

KONDITOURS GALORE. Karl Schwager had recruited a staff of meister konditours to start The Swiss Colony Bakery on its road to success. The first crew included, from left to right, (first row)

GINGERBREAD MEN, ALL. By 1973, some konditours had left and more had joined the staff, bringing the total to nine. Here they are shown with gingerbread characters they created. From left to right are Horst Hart, Gerhardt Kasinger, Erich Westphal, Franz Engesser, Werner Siegel,

Josef Nussbaumer, Franz Rastbaumwieser, Karl Schwager, Horst Hart, and Kurt Sebek; (second row) Walter Bruckmiller, Werner Siegel, Hans Koch, and Joe Berger.

Kurt Sebek, Josef Nussbaumer, Hans Koch, and Franz Rastbaumwieser. (Wisconsin State Journal photograph by Edwin Stein.)

TALENTED BAKERS. Many of the konditours went on to become important to The Swiss Colony matrix. Horst Hart eventually became the chief food stylist for the Photo Studio. Here he is erecting a 1979 catalog cover shot of gingerbread pieces. Josef Nussbaumer shifted to the Resource Planning Department, Franz Rastbaumwieser became manager of the Bakery Research Kitchen, and Franz Engesser became production scheduler for the entire The Swiss Colony Bakery, a position he holds yet today.

Huge Ovens Welcomed. Bakery production became much more efficient and able to produce larger quantities of baked goods with the acquisition and installation of two 60-foot band ovens. These ovens featured moving stainless steel conveyers that carried various items through temperature and time zones for the best finished product. The first oven was installed in 1979.

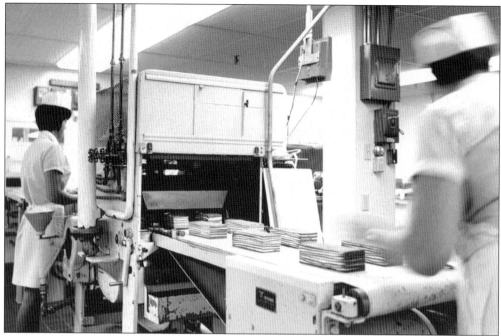

YOU'VE COME A LONG WAY, BABY! By the time this photograph was taken in 1970, enrobing machines had taken the drudgery out of encasing dobosh tortes and other bakery items in chocolate. (Courtesy Northern Natural Gas Company publication *Transmission*.)

PUMPING CHOCOLATE. Originally, the bakery used chocolate in solid 10-pound blocks, which needed to be melted and tempered before use. Installation of heated tanks, which could hold thousands of gallons of liquid chocolate, brought more efficiency. One of the first tanker-truck loads of chocolate in this form is being unloaded here. Shown are, from left to right, two unidentified Ambrosia Chocolate Company employees, and Evan Chambers and Karl Schwager from The Swiss Colony.

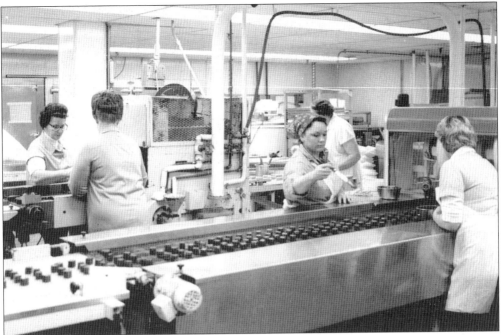

CHOCOLATE COATERS. By the late 1970s, new enrobing machines streamlined operations even further. Using the liquid chocolate pumped from the holding tanks to the enrobers allowed 70,000 petits fours a day to be coated with luxury chocolate. Horst Hart had produced 60,000 petits fours by hand in all of 1961.

INTRICATE DECORATING. After enrobing, the petits fours were hand decorated by skilled decorators. Much testing by bakery engineers on automated decorating equipment indicated that nothing could replicate the human hand. So the tradition of hand decorating continued and is still used today by associates whose skill level in applying these motifs is unequalled anywhere.

CHARACTERS ARRIVE. Not all of the chocolate is used to encase baked product, though. Solid chocolate characters were designed and became features on catalog pages. "Chris Mouse" was a favorite with children. Here Betsy Gavigan (left) and Helen Martin apply decorations.

A CLOSE-UP OF DECORATING. A letter to The Swiss Colony from December 26, 1979, states: "Dear Sir. Please send me the cost of a chocolate Chris Mouse. My little brother and me ate my sister's mouse and I have to replace it. He ate most of it—I just had a little. N.D.W., Great Falls, Montana."

AUTOMATION. Even though The Swiss Colony Bakery utilizes many employees in its production area, there is a lot of efficient equipment needed to produce all the items featured in a catalog. This overall view of the production area gives one an idea of the various pieces of equipment utilized. The bakery employs associates on three shifts to meet demand for products.

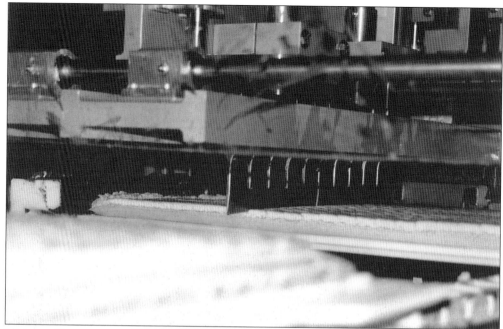

MODERN TECHNOLOGY. The photographs on these two pages show how cutting-edge technology is utilized in modern-day facilities. This view is of an ultrasonic cutter slicing through product. Sound waves induced on the cutting blade allow for a clean cut, with little tearing of the product.

PICK AND PLACE. This equipment picks up individual petits fours after they have been cut from a larger cake sheet utilizing a high-velocity water jet and transports and places them on a moving belt that carries them through an enrobing machine. Countless hours of hand labor are saved with this system.

TRUFFLES GALORE. A depositing machine forms and drops perfectly shaped truffles of various flavors onto plastic sheets. Once cooled, the truffles are then given a coat of luxury chocolate, decorated, and boxed for eager customers.

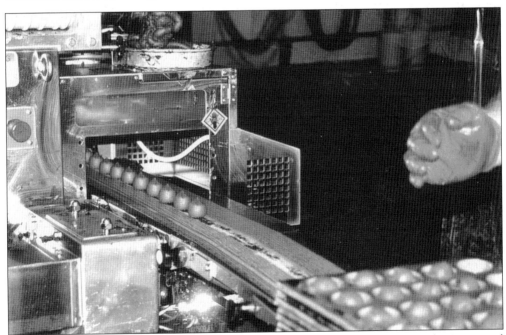

TWO FLAVORS AT ONCE! The bakery's Rheon equipment allows the injection of one material or flavor inside another. This shows brownie pockets being formed. The machine automatically places caramel, in this instance, inside a brownie batter, which is then placed in cupcake-like tins and baked for an unusual and delicious treat.

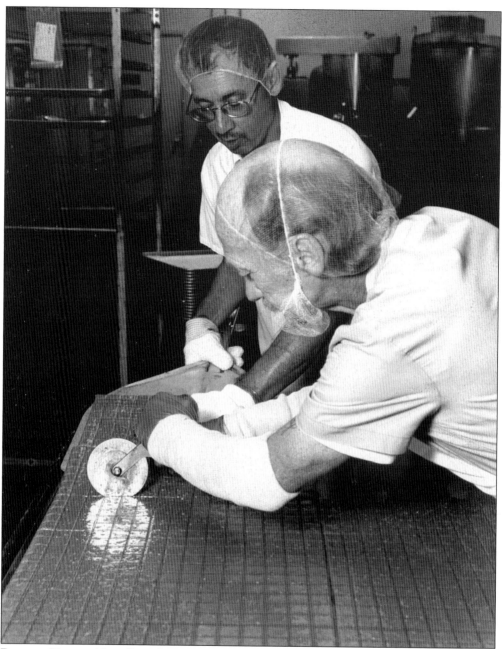

BUTTER TOFFEE. Not all products can be mechanized. Old-fashioned butter toffee has to be cooked in copper kettles and then, at the right moment, turned out on a cooling table, spread in a thin sheet, and cut into pieces. Here Tom Fey (rear) and Jim Messel cut the still-hot toffee into pieces. It is then chocolate coated and dusted with nuts.

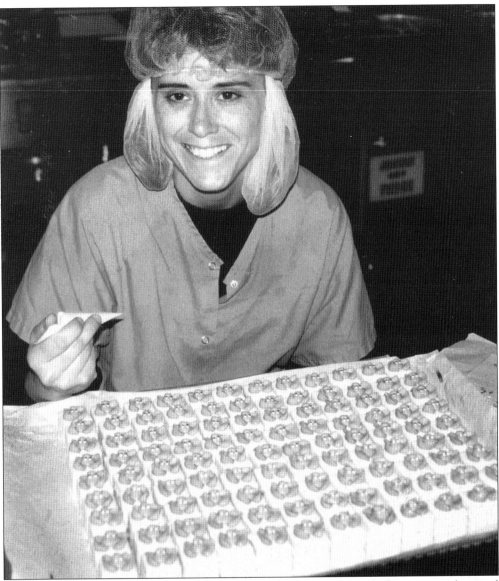

HAND DECORATION. The incredible skill of workers in the bakery results in cute, whimsical goodies. Here Sue Phillips decorates the tops of larger petits fours with an elephant decoration.

HOUSE PARTS. Gingerbread has been a mainstay of the bakery for many years. By 1982, mechanization allowed the bakery to form gingerbread house pieces by machine. A conveyor carried the pieces right into the band oven. With the then-new OKA press are, from left to right, an unidentified manufacturer's representative, bakery manager Gary Kappe, and Renita Coyle (née Meinert).

SUGAR AND SPICE. Gingerbread houses are decorated in a variety of formats. Here Sharon Buri applies icing to a house under construction. Racks of gingerbread houses make a fitting background. Gingerbread production had reached 200,000 units per year by the late 1970s.

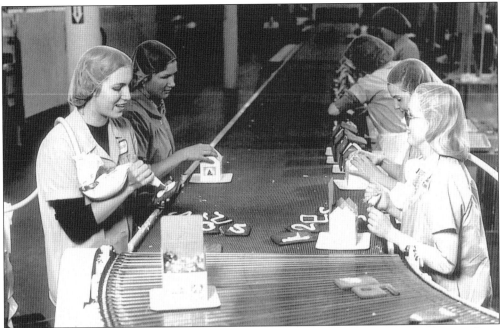

HOUSE CONSTRUCTION. Gingerbread parts are applied to a form as the houses move down a conveyer belt. Decoration and candy application are added farther down the line. These construction engineers are Joan Walters (left rear), Heidi Lacy (left front), Deb Allen (right rear), and an unidentified woman (right front).

A SUBDIVISION! The bakery hand decorates a small city of gingerbread houses every year to delight both children and grown-ups every Christmas. The workers are unidentified.

An Elaborate House. Not all the gingerbread houses produced make their way to customers. Gwen Connolly of the Bakery Research Kitchen constructs an intricate and highly decorated version every year. The house greets visitors to The Swiss Colony as they enter the main reception area.

Hand Decoration. The intricate decorations on Swiss Colony products show up everywhere. The company's famous red velvet cake gets a bouquet of roses on top. Yes, the cakes are hand frosted, too.

RESEARCH. Many of The Swiss Colony's innovative products are the result of many hours of incredibly detailed research work. Dan Moats, a master baker, works on cookie variations here. Moats was the youngest baker ever to earn a master baker's designation in the United States.

IT IS VERY BIG! From left to right, Kurt Sebek, Franz Engesser, and Josef Nussbaumer created this 260-pound, 48-inch cheesecake in July 1976. The 250,000-calorie delicacy was used to promote the 10th anniversary of a Swiss Colony store in Wichita, Kansas.

BEEHIVE. The bakery area is buzzing with activity year-round as various baked goods are combined into gift packages. This 1965 photograph shows a packing line in operation.

MANY AWARDS. The bakery division has garnered many Wisconsin Department of Agriculture awards over the years for its products, which are judged by consumers at the Wisconsin State Fair. In this photograph, the 1993 Alice in Dairyland, Angela Tuthills (née Corbin), presents two awards to Jim Glessner (left), the author of this book, and Franz Rastbaumwieser.

Three

ITS FOLKS ARE ITS GREATEST ASSET

The single thing that has made The Swiss Colony what it is today is all the people that work here. I am continually amazed at the 'responsibility factor.' People put in hours way above what is required. It has always been that way. People have made the company what it is today.
—Robert Ableman, vice chairman, 2001

FOUNDER OF THE SWISS COLONY, RAY KUBLY. Kubly was an exceedingly thorough individual. Robert Ableman, company vice chairman, recalls, "Ray called me one morning about a tax problem. We talked about 10–15 minutes, and I said I'd get the answer. He called again mid-morning and we talked about five minutes and he had another question. He called again about noon and we were off on another tangent. Finally he called again about 5 p.m. to resolve the latest question. The first call was from Monroe; the second from Chicago; the third from Las Vegas; and the final one from Los Angeles . . . all the same day. Ray could not let go of a question until he had an answer."

MARGUERITE KUBLY. Her name was Marguerite Kubly, but her friends called her Peg, and the customers with whom she corresponded called her Maggie. She married Ray Kubly on July 3, 1931, about five years after Ray started The Swiss Colony. Following the birth of their two sons, Peg became involved in the day-to-day operations of the fledgling company. Her personal touch, which was a friendlier manner than the business practices of the day, led to the genuine concern for the people philosophy that the company follows to this day. That customer philosophy is indicated by the correspondence The Swiss Colony receives that are not orders, but of a personal nature. Those amounted to two-thirds of a million pieces of mail in 1995!

PAT KUBLY. Now company chairman, Pat is the first son of Ray and Peg Kubly. Pat and his brother, Mike, both worked summers and Christmases at entry level jobs from an early age, through high school and college years. As a physics and mathematics major, Pat intended to be a scientist. But, after an Air Force stint, he came back to The Swiss Colony in 1957. When his father finally began working at the company full time in 1961, father and son made a pretty good team. When Ray succumbed to a heart attack in 1968, the young Pat took over the company's reins. Today he guides a multifaceted direct marketing conglomerate still headquartered in Monroe.

A FINAL APPROVAL. An executive marketing group reviews layouts for the catalogs. They include, from left to right, Ryan Kubly, director of strategic planning; John Baumann, The Swiss Colony president; Ann Bush, vice president of merchandising and inventory management for The Swiss Colony; and Pat Kubly, company chairman. Ryan Kubly is a grandson of founder Ray Kubly and the third generation of Kublys within The Swiss Colony.

STYLISH THEN. Ray Kubly was born on a dairy farm in Clarno Township, south of Monroe, on September 3, 1901. This photograph, from around 1905, shows the young entrepreneur in clothing that was the style of the time.

UNIVERSITY STUDENT. A dapper young Ray Kubly was in style with the times, as shown by this photograph from around 1926. Ray had been a star "two-miler" on the University of Wisconsin track team at Madison during the years following his transfer there from Lawrence College in Appleton.

SHIPPING CHEESE. Ray Kubly (second from right) was a man of determination. When he made up his mind to find customers around the country for Green County's finest cheeses, he found a way. Here, with some of the early shipments from Monroe's Milwaukee Road Depot, he and his brother, Glenn (in other white jacket), pose with a package to a customer. The two men flanking the brothers are unidentified.

A GIFT SELECTION. By 1961, The Swiss Colony had branched into decorative Christmas packaging and gifts. Ray Kubly is pictured with a display of some of them. The original folk art paintings by Carl Marty, an early Swiss cheese pioneer, grace the walls of the office. These paintings are still treasured by The Swiss Colony and remain on display at its Monroe facility.

DINING IN CHICAGO. This family photograph shows young Pat (left) and Mike with parents Peg and Ray Kubly. The youngsters worked at many company jobs when not in school. The family is

dining at the Bismark Hotel in Chicago. Today Pat is the company chairman and Mike, a retired surgeon in Milwaukee, is a director of the company.

STILL GOING STRONG. Forrest Kubly, Ray's younger brother, has been involved in the day-to-day operation of the company since the late 1930s. His area of expertise was in cheese buying, but he was responsible for the purchasing of all production materials prior to the 1960s.

ENTERTAINING A BUYER. Wholesale marketing of cheese was also undertaken. From left to right, Tom Hartwig, Walt Donovan, and Forrest Kubly entertain an unidentified cheese buyer (on the far right) from the West Coast.

STARTED BAKERY. Karl Schwager was the first of three generations of Schwagers to be associated with The Swiss Colony. Schwager was head steward on the famous "Super Chief" train, a position where he spent most of his professional career. He came to Monroe when Ray Kubly bought his club cheese business in Forest Park, Illinois, called Chalet Cheese. Schwager was part of the deal and was known as the father of The Swiss Colony Bakery operation.

MARKETING ICON. Kurt Schwager, son of Karl, came to Monroe initially to operate the Chalet Cheese business, which The Swiss Colony had purchased. He became involved with developing a variety of "wine" cheeses and then was asked to assist in the office. Kurt then became involved in marketing, catalog production, and magazine advertising. He was senior vice president when he retired and passed away in 2003.

OPERATIONS CHIEF. Robert Ableman, now company vice chairman, had a background in financial accounting and was associated with a local accounting firm that did work for The Swiss Colony. In 1974, he was asked to join The Swiss Colony on a full-time basis and became executive vice president, essentially responsible for the day-to-day operations of the firm.

IMPORTANT EXECUTIVES. Three "stars" of The Swiss Colony production operations are shown here. These three vice presidents, Earl Hager (top left), Perry Power (top right), and Werner Weissenfluh (bottom), all involved in different areas of the company, were important contributors to the success of the business.

FIRST EMPLOYEE. At the 1996 retirement party, John Chambers (right) received a Lifetime Achievement Award honoring him as The Swiss Colony's first employee. Chambers worked part or full time for the company from 1932 until his retirement in 1987. CEO Pat Kubly personally congratulated Chambers and presented the award.

BIG BIRTHDAY. The oldest living Swiss Colony retiree, Nora Rubi, was honored in 2005 at the retirement party. Rubi celebrated her 100th birthday earlier that year. She started with the company in 1936, working on and off until her retirement in 1980.

BADGER BOOSTER DAYS. This annual fund-raiser for the University of Wisconsin-Madison Athletic Department was started in 1954 by Ray Kubly. The tradition continues with Pat Kubly (right) and wife Shirley Kubly (left). They flank the late Elroy "Crazylegs" Hirsch and his wife, Ruth. Elroy, a former football great at the Universities of Wisconsin and Michigan, went on to become an NFL immortal with the Los Angeles Rams. Later in his colorful career, he served as the athletic director of the University of Wisconsin from 1969 until 1987.

CHRISTMAS FUN. One of the ways the company tries to keep the spirit of Christmas alive among its own ranks is by having a company-wide Christmas decorating contest. It is a huge morale booster when employees need it most: at the height of the busy season. Here are two Santas and their jolly crew of helpers, portrayed by company employees. From left to right are (first row) Sheila Berrey, Deb Weis, and Mary Mau; (second row) George Schutte, Chris Mouse, Kelly Metz (an employee's child), and Jerry Lokken.

SPORTS ENTHUSIASTS. Swiss Colony–sponsored sports teams help employees develop a friendship and camaraderie beyond their coworker status. This 1991 softball team includes, from left to right, (first row) Jon Schye, Carl Murray, Bryan Buri, Ken Hill, and Kirk Davies; (second row) Bill Hermanson, Larry Green, Bill Barnes, Tom Kellen, and Andy Sefcik.

COMMUNITY OUTREACH. Lori Giese (rear), from the Systems and Programming Department, is surrounded by bright young faces while teaching Junior Achievement classes at Parkside School in Monroe in 2004. The third graders learned about how society works from a business perspective. The Swiss Colony supports the program by purchasing materials and providing employees to lead class discussions.

ONE MILLION HOURS! Safety is emphasized at The Swiss Colony. The bakery division reached a landmark safety record without a lost-time accident. Employees were rewarded with a steak dinner served by the executive staff. Bakery vice president Art Bartsch, with dark glasses in the background, thanked employees for efforts in attaining the goal. The Mailing Department for the Swiss Colony companies handled 36 million pieces of mail in 2002 without a single lost-time accident. That was the 10th year in a row that department achieved this safety award.

BOOSTER DISCOUNT CERTIFICATES. The company has an unusual incentive program. It features certificates presented to employees for recognition and rewards for achievements above and beyond the norm. Here Esther Stephens (left), corporate upsell (add-on sales in addition to a customer's original order) coordinator, presents Clinton, Iowa, Contact Center's Donna Schoenfeld with some booster certificates. Employees can use these for product purchases and the like.

HELPING THOSE IN NEED. Swiss Colony employee Jennie Crase challenged those in her group to compete against other company departments in a scavenger hunt to accumulate items for food pantries and the troops in Iraq. The resource planning group took first place in the competition, contributing 17.5 items per person. From left to right are Beth Hellwig, Sharon Drews, Judy Waelti, and Dave Down.

HURRICANE RELIEF. While visiting the Hannibal, Missouri, Contact Center, a data center affiliate, for an open house in 2005, company president John Baumann was presented with contributions from Hannibal employees for Hurricane Katrina relief. Shown are, from left to right, Paula Hulse, Carole McKenzie, Baumann, Deb Bird, Carol Murphy, and Susan Fohey. Employee donations from all locations were matched by The Swiss Colony for a total relief donation of $24,294.10.

BUSINESS ETHICS AWARD. Swiss Colony president John Baumann (right) displays the award The Swiss Colony received in 2003 from the Madison, Wisconsin, Chapter of the Society of Financial Service Professionals. The company was nominated for the award by Monroe businessman Dave Mosher (left). Edgewood College associate professor Elaine Beaubien defined business ethics: "Working ethically means doing everything as if your mother is looking over your shoulder and you want to make her proud."

WELLNESS. Because wellness is an important goal with the company, employees received a pedometer at the annual corporate meeting in 2005. They kept track of steps walked, doing 5,000 steps per day minimum. The symbolic goal was to walk to all corporate locations within a year. By June 16, 2005, they should have reached Dickeyville, Wisconsin. Employees there to greet them were, from left to right, (first row) Dianna Richardson, Deb Obershaw, Sue Knief, Sharon Selchert, and Lloyd Meng; (second row) Sharon Klein, Linda Schneider, Sue Droessler, Deb Stacher, Candace Roberts, and Lorie Schwalenberg.

FINDING EMPLOYEES. Since Swiss Colony companies need to recruit almost 6,000 temporary employees at various locations during the holiday rush, Public Relations and Human Resource Departments take traveling exhibits to county fairs, festivals, and community events. Event attendees can sign up for prizes (above) or to be contacted for employment opportunities.

DAIRY MONTH PROMOTER. Over the years, many famous personalities have found an association with The Swiss Colony. Here comedian Joey Bishop poses with this Swiss Colony wheel of Swiss to promote June Dairy Month in 1968.

LIONS LIKE CHEESE. Melvin Laird, then a United States representative and later secretary of defense in the Richard Nixon administration from 1969 to 1973, was joined by Alice in Dairyland (left) and Miss Wisconsin (right), both unidentified, in this early-1960s photograph. The occasion was the Lions' International Convention at the Palmer House in Chicago. The Swiss Colony had sent a giant wheel of Swiss cheese for the event.

ALICE MAKES A VISIT. Forrest Kubly, who celebrated his 90th birthday in 2005, is still active with the company. The younger brother of company founder Ray, Forrest is pictured in 1953 with Alice in Dairyland, Mary Ellen Jordal (née Jenks) of Edina, Minnesota, who later became vice president for Green Giant Company and Pillsbury Company.

THE GOVERNOR TOURS. Tommy Thompson, then governor of Wisconsin, paid a visit to The Swiss Colony Bakery in 1990. Employee Kathy Nipple is weighing bakery product. Thompson more recently went on to serve nationally as secretary of Health and Human Services in the first presidential administration of George W. Bush.

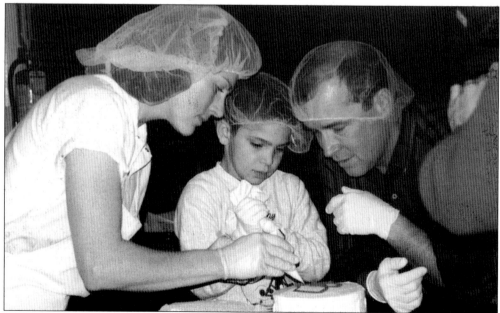

HARDER THAN IT LOOKS. The Swiss Colony Bakery was highlighted in 1995 when Madison-located WISC-TV's John Karcher brought a young guest, Justin, from his Wednesday's Child program for a visit. Dawn Ditzenberger gave them both some decorating tips.

MANY LONGTIME EMPLOYEES. Swiss Colony employees have a tradition of company longevity. Eleanor Smith, systems and programming, has been with the company since 1965 and was recognized in 2005 on her 40th anniversary. A search of company records revealed that in late 2005 there were 318 employees, permanent and temporary, who had worked for the company for 20 years or more!

A FAMILY AFFAIR. Esther Stephens (left) of the Contact Center administration celebrated her 35th year with the company in 2005. Working for The Swiss Colony is a family affair with this group. Esther's husband, Les (right), works in messenger services; daughter Becky Henke is a director of food merchandising; and son Mike Stephens works in maintenance.

CHEESE DAYS. Monroe's every-other-year celebration of local cheese heritage played an important role in The Swiss Colony growth. An early parade float features Hans and Maggie and cheese gifts. In 1950, Swiss Colony sandwich crews assembled 60,000 cheese sandwiches to sell and distribute free at the event.

CROWD-PLEASER. The Swiss Colony parade float has gone through many changes over the years. The most recent version features two huge kid-pleasers: a gingerbread house and that lovable Chris Mouse. The mid-September festival continues to draw 100,000 visitors into Monroe, which only has a population of 11,000.

Four

FISH BAIT AND LIMBURGER TO THE MAGIC OF CHRISTMAS

Marketing Plans for Ray Kubly's upstart company may have had a noticeable "bump"
when on Nov. 1, 1926, Green County Swiss cheese was named the nation's best—awarded
gold and silver at the 1926 National Dairy Show.
—Item from the Monroe Evening Times

Prices effective Apr. 18, 1927. Prices subject to change without notice.

ORDER BLANK FOR SPECIAL PARCEL POST PACKAGE

To GREEN COUNTY CHEESE CO., Monroe, Wis.:

Kindly find enclosed $............................ for which please send me family cheese package I have checked. Postage prepaid.

Round Swiss Cheese, 4 pounds	$2.00
Round Swiss Cheese, Prime cut 2 pounds	$1.10
Brick Cheese, full Brick, 5 pounds	$1.50
Limburg, two cakes—four pounds	$1.20
Limburg, two cakes, two pounds	$0.75
American, 5 lb. box in tinfoil	$1.75
Pimento, 5 lb. box in tinfoil	$1.85

We guarantee that the stock will be of the best quality Green County production.

SIGN HERE ....

Complete address,
Street and number ....

Post Office ....

GOLDEN CHEESE FROM DAIRYLAND

ONE OF THE FIRST ADVERTISEMENTS. Ray Kubly began the marketing of cheese on a really small scale. The top order blank is from The Swiss Colony's second year of operation. It was simple and straightforward. Postcards with the addition of a photograph of wheels of Swiss and the "Little Switzerland" logo appeared shortly thereafter. Note that in addition to "summer cured Swiss," Port Salut and cheddar varieties had been added to the offering.

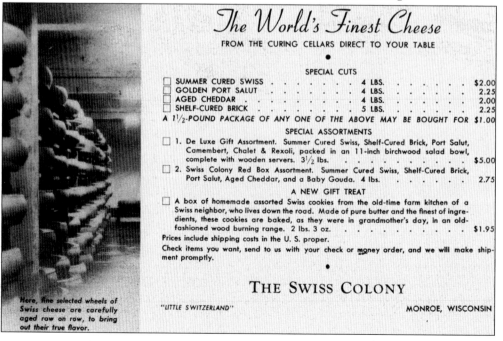

The World's Finest Cheese

FROM THE CURING CELLARS DIRECT TO YOUR TABLE

•

SPECIAL CUTS

☐ SUMMER CURED SWISS	4 LBS.	$2.00
☐ GOLDEN PORT SALUT	4 LBS.	2.25
☐ AGED CHEDDAR	4 LBS.	2.00
☐ SHELF-CURED BRICK	5 LBS.	2.25

A 1½-POUND PACKAGE OF ANY ONE OF THE ABOVE MAY BE BOUGHT FOR $1.00

SPECIAL ASSORTMENTS

☐ 1. De Luxe Gift Assortment. Summer Cured Swiss, Shelf-Cured Brick, Port Salut, Camember, Chalet & Rexoli, packed in an 11-inch birchwood salad bowl, complete with wooden servers. 3½ lbs. $5.00

☐ 2. Swiss Colony Red Box Assortment. Summer Cured Swiss, Shelf-Cured Brick, Port Salut, Aged Cheddar, and a Baby Gouda. 4 lbs. 2.75

A NEW GIFT TREAT

☐ A box of homemade assorted Swiss cookies from the old-time farm kitchen of a Swiss neighbor, who lives down the road. Made of pure butter and the finest of ingredients, these cookies are baked, as they were in grandmother's day, in an old-fashioned wood burning range. 2 lbs. 3 oz. $1.95

Prices include shipping costs in the U. S. proper.

Check items you want, send to us with your check or money order, and we will make shipment promptly.

•

THE SWISS COLONY

"LITTLE SWITZERLAND"

MONROE, WISCONSIN

Here, fine selected wheels of Swiss cheese are carefully aged row on row, to bring out their true flavor.

December 5, 1939

Dear Friend:

    Solve your gift problem simply, quickly. . .

    with fine, rare fully-aged cheese in gay Christmas assortments. It's a gift that's in good taste, one that will be appreciated by everyone on your Christmas list.

    And that's what The Swiss Colony offers you. . . cheese that is truly unusual in quality, unlike any you can buy at a store. Months and months ago the aged cheese that goes into our assortments was set aside because of its especially fine quality, and cured in curing rooms which years of experience have found ideal for the development of fine flavor.

    So when your friends receive The Swiss Colony cheese assortments you may be sure they are really receiving what we Swiss consider the very finest cheese in the world.

    Enclosed is a folder that gives you the prices on our renowned gift packages. Use the enclosed order form or write us a letter and send us your mailing list and enclosures. We will take care of the rest. Do it now and get your Christmas gift problems settled!

                   Very truly yours,

M. W. Kubly

                   THE SWISS COLONY at
                   Monroe, Wisconsin

P. S. Be sure to include an assortment for your own use, too. Give yourself and your family a treat.

    Phone Monroe 67.

TELLING THE STORY. By 1939, an introductory letter had been added to the selling folder. It touted the fine quality of cheese. Note the interesting phone number at the bottom of the letter. It was during that 1930s era that the Wisconsin state legislature required hotels and restaurants to serve two-thirds of an ounce of Wisconsin cheese and butter with meals costing 25¢ or more! That law has long since expired but serves to illustrate the pride that the state had, and has, in its dairy industry. The Kublys recognized that pride and carried it into sales literature.

CHEESE VARIETIES. This photograph shows an early crate of Swiss Colony cheese selections. Included were Camembert, a lunch cheese, Old Heidelberg (a type of liederkranz), and Limburger. The odiferous Limburger was, and is, a favorite of the Swiss and German residents of Green County, where Monroe is located. It had its origins in Europe, and its recipe was brought to America with immigrants. It still boasts many connoisseurs, and the only cheese factory still making Limburger in the United States is located in Green County.

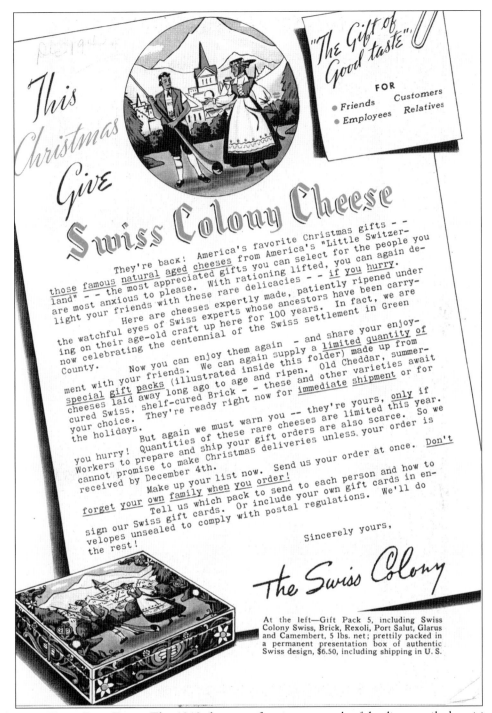

A 1940s Four-Page Flyer. This 1940s four-page flyer is an example of the direct mail advertising The Swiss Colony used to "grow" its business over the years. An early rendition of Hans and Maggie graces the cover. On the back, copy advised customers, "Cheese is a Victory Food; Eat It Often, Says Uncle Sam." The Peasant Box shown in the lower corner was a customer favorite during those years. A larger rendition of the Peasant Box is shown on page 81.

IN FORTUNE MAGAZINE. Another technique invented and used in 1940 was the narrative format. This advertisement appeared in the November 1940 issue of *Fortune* magazine. The photographs in the advertisement show the dairy farm, the cheese maker, and the Swiss cheese undergoing the aging process. The prose in a portion of the advertisement states, "You would like our picturesque Turner Hall, built in the style of the homeland. Here you see the old-time schottische, waltz and polka, danced to the music of the zither and accordion; young men and their *maidli*, old men and their *frauen* yodeling ancient airs you probably never heard before."

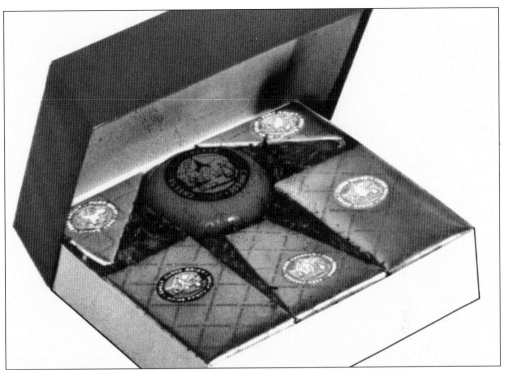

THE RED BOX OF CHEESE. This was one of The Swiss Colony's early best sellers. It was such a mainstay of the business it was pictured on one of the parade floats in an early Monroe Cheese Days festival. In 1949, this four-pound version sold for $4.55. Peg Kubly designed this package.

THE PEASANT BOX. It followed the Red Box success and was a creation of Peg Kubly and Raymond Loewy and Associates. This design inspired the Hans and Maggie logo that The Swiss Colony still uses today. Turn to page 91 for a look at the early and current logos. Both gifts appeared in advertising literature as early as 1948.

AND IT WORKED. They say the proof of the bait was in its huge catches. This 37-pound yellow catfish was caught in Lake Fort Phantom-Hill in Abilene, Texas, on May 6, 1949, by C. L. Williams of Avoca, Texas. Note the can of Monroe catfish bait near the monster's head. The bait was retailed by Sears, Montgomery Ward, and other retailers.

82

GIFTS OF PERFECT TASTE. By the 1950s, The Swiss Colony was branching into small catalogs to reach its mail-order customers. This is the cover page of a 1951 version, where the "Gifts of Perfect Taste" signature is already being used. The 16-page booklet still contained the original Red Box and Peasant Box gifts.

THE FAMOUS PLACE ORDERS. Another way The Swiss Colony used its catalogs was to list the names of celebrities who had ordered gifts. This is the inside back cover page of the booklet shown above. Notables who had ordered included Mrs. Franklin D. Roosevelt, Bud Abbott, Katharine Cornell, Sen. and Mrs. J. W. Fulbright, John M. Golden, Helen Hayes, Ronald Reagan, Ginger Rogers, James Stewart, Rudy Vallee, and Fibber McGee and Molly.

Here are a few of our celebrated Swiss Colony customers:

MRS. FRANKLIN D. ROOSEVELT
MR. BUD ABBOTT
MISS KATHARINE CORNELL
SENATOR AND MRS. J. W. FULBRIGHT
MR. JOHN M. GOLDEN
MISS HELEN HAYES
MR. RONALD REAGAN
MISS GINGER ROGERS
MR. JAMES STEWART
MR. RUDY VALLEE
FIBBER McGEE & MOLLY

Swiss Colony gifts are available all year 'round for special gift occasions.

Prices include delivery anywhere in the United States.

GUARANTEE: We are proud of the reputation that 26 years as the leading mail order cheese house has given us — a reputation for reliability and for gifts of superlative quality beautifully packed and carefully shipped. Every gift we send out is guaranteed to be just as it is represented in this catalog, and to be delivered in perfect condition to any address in the United States.

Our reference: The Commercial and Savings Bank, Monroe, Wisconsin

THE ENCLOSED ORDER BLANK WILL GIVE YOU SUGGESTIONS FOR ORDERING SWISS COLONY GIFTS THE EASY WAY.

Send checks or money orders payable to

The Swiss Colony
MONROE, WISCONSIN

Games CHEST

An *impressive* gift, designed by Raymond Loewy Associates. It's fit for a castle or a country home — will glorify a yacht or a hunting cabin. Here's good fun plus fabulous food. For checkers and backgammon: a board, red and white interlocking checkers, dice and 2 dice boxes. For canasta: cards, basket, magnetized score pad and pencil.

All this and choice cheese, too . . . June-cured Swiss, Sharp Aged Cheddar, Aged American, Brick, Port Salut, Blue Cheese, a Gouda, and a crock of Cheddar with Port Wine. *Available all year.*

Pack 18 — Games Chest with 8½ lbs. of cheese - - - - - delivered **$29.95**

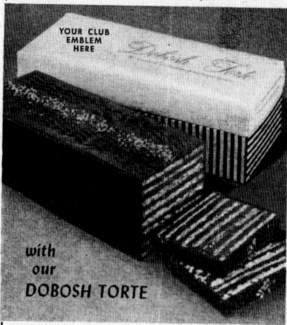
SALES OPPORTUNITIES. The evolving company, ever vigilant to sales opportunities, made a pitch for service club sales in the early 1960s. This advertisement, which appeared in *The Lion* magazine, used the company's famous signature dobosh torte as product. The venture did not reach expectations, however, and was discontinued.

"Cheese"

by

The Swiss Colony

New! Never Offered Before!

SAY CHEESE! Not all ventures were to become marketing successes either. In the late 1970s, a cheese club offer was designed. A journal was to be sent to club members six times a year with unique cheeses for sale from around the world. Discount certificates on selected cheeses were to be offered. The first issue was about to be mailed when company executives determined that the project probably would not succeed and dropped the project. This *"Cheese"* pamphlet has never been seen before by the general public.

JACK OWEN ENTERPRISES

CLIENT: THE SWISS COLONY
PRODUCT: CATALOG INQUIRY GENERATION
AS FILMED TV COMM'L NO: SCT-87-60-924
TITLE: "$24 VALUE"
DATE: 8/4/87
LENGTH: 60 SECONDS

1. CHEF: (VO) No, no, no!
LADY: (VO) Yes, yes, yes!

2. CHEF: How can you even think of giving away my famous Gingerbread House for free?

3. LADY: So more viewers will call The Swiss Colony's toll-free number

4. and ask for our free package of "3 Great Catalogs in One".

5. The Chocolate Shop...

6. The Gallery...

7. and our famous Christmas Gift Catalog...a 2 dollar value!

8. CHEF: They're free, too?
LADY: That's right...

9. but don't call yet, there's more.

10. CHEF: But why give away my 16 dollar Gingerbread House for free?

11. LADY: To get more people to sample our catalog products so they'll know how really good all our gifts are!

12. CHEF: Sample? The Gingerbread is my masterpiece. Why don't you give away a Petits Four?

13. LADY: Petits Fours? That's a great idea! If you call right now,

14. we'll send you 6 dollars worth of delicious Petits Fours

15. plus this sensational 16 dollar Gingerbread House ... both free with your first order

16. from any of our 3 free catalogs...

17. a 24 dollar value yours free with just a toll-free call.

18. 1-800-356-9000.

19. LADY: Now, you can call!

20. 1-800-356-9000.

A TELEVISION ADVERTISEMENT. As the company progressed into the 1980s, an effort was initiated to lure new buyers to The Swiss Colony line of products. This storyboard of a television one-minute commercial was designed by Jack Owen Enterprises and featured master pastry chef Horst Hart. The lighthearted banter about "free" products and a toll-free number to call inspired many new customers.

CHRIS MOUSE ARRIVES.
The lovable Chris Mouse figure was designed in 1958 by artist Helen Endres (above). A renowned artist, Endres's illustrations appear on many of the beautiful tins that contain Swiss Colony products. These may be seen on page 90. A contest to name the mascot in 1977 resulted in a tie. Two employees, Lynn Gnatzig and Becky Aurit, came up with the same name. Over the years, Chris has appeared in a multitude of poses and costumes. The rendition in the photograph at right was printed on place mats used at the Swiss Colony Inn restaurant in Monroe. The depiction as Wilhelm Tell was entirely intentional.

A MOUSE IN THE BAKERY. Helen Endres continued to depict Chris Mouse in a variety of poses. This is one of several large circle paintings that adorn the walls of The Swiss Colony Bakery administrative area. Chris is shown in a chef's toque, painting decorations on dobosh tortes.

THE TEACHER! Chris eventually progressed into a more human form, and Swiss Colony employees get a chance to portray Chris at various events. In this lighthearted portrait, Chris teaches company president John Baumann all the intricacies of product and packaging. Baumann also holds one of the authentic Swiss alpenhorns that grace the walls of the reception area in the main offices.

COLLECTIBLES. For many years, the company has designed very colorful and attractive tins as collectible containers for bakery products. The Chris Mouse mascot, in a variety of depictions, is used on many of them. Other favorite themes are of Currier and Ives, Santa, and local scenes such as the local courthouse and a restored early-Monroe mansion. This collection of tins shows some of the intricate and beautiful designs.

HANS AND MAGGIE. This is one of the early renditions of the Hans and Maggie logo used on company products. The Peasant Box design was the basis for it. Later it was revised, stylized, and modernized into the logo of the present day, shown below.

COLORFUL MARKETERS. Direct marketing tools offered by The Swiss Colony and its affiliates include this selection of catalogs produced during 2005.

Five

THE MAIL-ORDER ROAD LEADS TO NATIONWIDE RETAIL

Combined with Christmas kiosks in some malls, the stores were a growing concern throughout the late 1970s, topping out in 1982 with 225 locations all across the nation.
—Ailsa Thalacker, Swiss Colony stores

At State Fair. This Swiss Colony Chalet was built at the Wisconsin State Fair in Milwaukee in 1948. "America's Dairyland" was celebrating its centennial year and The Swiss Colony joined in the celebration with yodelers, bell ringers, horn blowers, and plenty of Swiss cheese. Three of the 29 hostesses wore original Swiss Bernese festival dresses worth $500 each (in 1948)!

The Swiss Colony Inn. Monroe's inn, pictured here in 1985, had been rebuilt after a fire destroyed much of it in 1965. It closed in 1986. The inn was a favorite restaurant with many Monroe area residents and also sold a wide selection of Swiss Colony products.

FIRST STORE. Helen Stauffer was one of the early employees of the very first Swiss Colony store. Swiss Colony Stores, affiliate, largely credited with identifying The Swiss Colony to the general buying public across the nation, peaked in 1982.

FORERUNNER. This is an early, typical Swiss Colony store, which dotted shopping malls across the United States.

FRANCHISING. The company looked to the franchising technique to grow its market presence. This 1967 advertisement touted the opportunity to own a franchise retail store. Ultimately, it was determined to shut down franchise operations and concentrate on other marketing opportunities.

A MALL PRESENCE. These two views of the Swiss Colony retail store in West Towne Mall in Madison, Wisconsin, show how the concept and motif of the retail stores had changed by 1985. "Lease-lining" was a popular sales technique at the stores, where employees would offer samples of Swiss Colony products to mall shoppers in an effort to induce product sales.

NOW THAT IS A BIG CHEESE. The 600-pound mammoth Wisconsin cheddar in this photograph was used for a Swiss Colony Stores promotion in the early 1970s. The pretty Swiss lass is unidentified.

IT IS PARTY TIME. From left to right, Fran Hartwig, Sue Jacobson, and Marianne Rasmussen, of the Swiss Colony outlet store, display their famous cheese trays in this 1991 photograph.

REAL CLASS. Green County Foods, a wholesale outgrowth of the franchising era, was marketing baked goods at the Fancy Food Show in San Francisco in 1999. Steve Janssen, tuxedo and all, is

showing the tuxedo collection of petits fours to interested buyers.

GENUINE SWISS TOUCH. Gottlieb Brandli, a well-known Old-World woodworker of the area, demonstrates how he carved designs for Swiss Colony gift boxes to Beth Roberts. Brandli, a Canton Zurich, Switzerland, native, made much of the furniture used in Swiss Colony franchise stores, even those in Hawaii and Alaska.

SAUSAGE KINGS. This 20-foot beef log was "rolled out" to celebrate new Swiss Colony stores in Atlanta, Georgia, and Lexington, Kentucky. Weighing in at 185 pounds, the novelty beef log was photographed with, from left to right, Dean Olson, Mike Bainbridge, Nate Bechtolt, Bill Lewis, Randy Bechtolt, Keith Andrews, and Larry Kundert.

Six

From Swiss to Sweaters, From Cheddar to Chaise Lounges

The Swiss Colony stopped being solely a food gift marketer years ago. Entrepreneurial spirit, along with the talent and desire to test, test, test, enabled us to greatly broaden our customer base. We truly want to play a part in our customers' lifestyle each and every day.
                    —Gary Schwager, president, Seventh Avenue, Inc.

THE EXPANSION BEGINS. The Swiss Colony's first nonfood catalog, Seventh Avenue, incorporated in 1986, was a big success when it premiered in 1982. Many more catalogs would follow, including Midnight Velvet in the fall of 1987 and incorporated in 1988. This photograph, from 1989, features employees involved in the development of that catalog. From left to right are Sheila Hobson, Jan Mathias, Peggy Frint, Becky Aurit, Ailsa Thalacker, and Sue Hall.

ASSOCIATES NEEDED. Growth in the nonfood area has created a need for merchandising managers and associates. Surrounded by product samples, this team closes a release of Through the Country Door catalog. From left to right are Mary Goeke, Carol Schmitz, Jill Hoogenakker, Sheila Hobson, Ann Bush, and Melissa Wuebben. Ann Bush is president of Through the Country Door, Inc., incorporated in 2000. The ratio of business from The Swiss Colony and affiliate company catalogs in 2005 was 80 percent sales from nonfood items and 20 percent from food items for the firm.

WORLD TRAVELERS. Merchandisers from various catalogs scour the world for unique consumer items. Here Christine Reese-Day, merchandiser for the nonfood group, connects with an unidentified manufacturer's representative in New York. Other merchandisers regularly travel to the Orient, India, Germany, and other countries to secure consumer goods for direct mail sales. Merchandisers spend 10 to 20 percent of their time on the road, also traveling extensively in the United States to locations like New York, Las Vegas, and Atlanta.

SELECTING THE MERCHANDISE. Once merchandise samples arrive, a team presents a "gift presentation" to executives to decide which items will appear in a particular catalog. Here, from left to right, Marcy Brayko, Charles Hemphill, Amanda Kloepping, and Joe Tomasiewicz review items.

How Will It Look? Selected items are then photographed and catalog page layouts created. Gary Schwager (center), vice president, marketing and publishing, looks on as Charles Hemphill (left) and Chris Vestin review layouts. The trio works in the new Inspiration Room, which has fabric-covered walls so a succession of layouts can be posted all around. Schwager is the third generation of his family to be associated with The Swiss Colony.

It Is All Digital. From the layouts, catalog pages are then created using highly advanced electronic publishing systems, where photographs and catalog copy are combined into attractive sales pages. Here Heidi Schneeberger (left) and Christy Simmer work on a Ginny's catalog cover.

A FINAL CHECK. One of the critical steps in assuring accurate representation on catalog pages is an actual comparison of merchandise to layouts and merchandise photographs. Scott Ballogh, with Quad Graphics (a firm that prints the catalogs), and Char Paulson from The Swiss Colony perform this important quality check. They especially compare colors from original products to the catalog representation.

MAKING LIFE EASIER. Ginny Bean, vice president, creative marketing services, is featured in some of the photograph layouts in the catalogs bearing her name. Bean is also involved in infomercials, a sales technique popular on various television channels. Bean is president of Ginny's, Inc., which was incorporated in 1990. A unique offering is a number of kitchen appliances that bear the Ginny's brand logo.

CUSTOMER PERSONALIZATION. An offering in some catalogs is personalization of clothing and other gift items. Here Jean Carber of the DeWitt, Iowa, fulfillment center operates the machine that adds embroidery to the items. Input to the equipment comes either from direct connection to a computer or through information contained on a small computer chip.

CUSTOM ENGRAVING. Another equipment piece at the DeWitt facility is an engraving machine. Wordage introduced via computer allows operator Kathy Hess to engrave as few as one or as many as 70 metal plates at once.

KEEPING TRACK OF IT ALL. Automated tracking of shipped packages is accomplished using a manifest system. Robin Bousselot (above) uses a handheld scanner to register an outgoing package. The system tracks everything from inventory to outgoing orders, seen progressing down a conveyer belt below. The DeWitt facility opened in 1995 and handles some of the shipping for nonfood catalog companies. Employment there is about 35 full-time and 250 part-time employees.

Seven

CUTTING-EDGE TECHNOLOGY SECURES THE FUTURE

Improving technology coupled with the ever-increasing skill sets of our members allows us to stretch our expertise into new frontiers. For example, our company boasts one of the most progressive database marketing teams in the direct marketing industry.
—John Baumann, president, The Swiss Colony, Inc.

IT WAS PAPER AND MORE PAPER. This photograph was taken in the old Knights of Columbus hall above the Citizen's Bank in Monroe sometime in the late 1940s. Seasonal help was housed in a number of different buildings around the community over the years. In the 1970s, the company also opened offices and a production area in Madison, Wisconsin.

NEILSEN SURVEYS. One of the jobs that kept employees of early data center operations busy was tabulating information from the Neilsen television surveys. This photograph, taken around 1966, shows employees editing the surveys before information was entered into the computer system via keypunching. Up to 4,000 survey "diaries" a day were processed.

THE PHONE IS RINGING. By 2001, six contact centers, under the jurisdiction of the affiliated SC Data Center, handled nearly four million phone calls a year. Contact centers are currently located in Monroe and Dickeyville, Wisconsin; Clinton, Iowa; and Hannibal, Missouri. All are connected to the Monroe computer mainframe for order processing.

SWISS ARMY. Wearing official Swiss Army caps, these employees take phone orders in addition to doing their regular jobs. Most full-time employees have been called upon to man the phones over the years during the crucial first week of December. From left to right are packing employees Patsy Broge, Uva Van Houten, and Clara Gill. Temporary employees throughout the community also help out by taking orders on their home computers, directly linked to the main computer.

HELPFUL ASSOCIATES. The Customer Service Department is an important link between The Swiss Colony and its customers. Highly trained technicians can tell customers what they ordered, where in the process the order is at, when it was shipped, or even change the order.

FOOD SAFETY. The Quality Assurance Department is a critical area of the food divisions. The Swiss Colony continually monitors all products for consumer safety. This photograph shows a testing procedure carried out by Jackie Cosgrove in an early laboratory area.

MODERN TESTING. The department is currently housed in its own facility where a team of lab technicians performs testing using the latest methods and equipment. This photograph shows Kathi Winker, quality assurance microbiologist, using a test strip containing less than one-eighth teaspoon of sample in an analyzer used to identify any potentially harmful bacteria.

NO NEGATIVES. Photography has seen a rapid technology progression. Early in catalog development, Swiss Colony products were transported to Chicago for photography. The resulting color negatives were utilized for printing. Here Horst Hart (left) and Jay Nelson evaluate negatives.

ADVANCING THE ART. In today's world, photography is accomplished digitally, using highly technical equipment. Here Stef Culberson, food stylist, fire glazes a ham in preparation for the shot. Photographer Ricky Christensen cleans off the foreground for the final photograph. The camera is visible on the right, and a preview of the ham photograph can be seen on the computer monitor. The images are transmitted electronically for layout and printing operations.

FROM CARDS TO BYTES. An area that has seen the greatest leap in technology over the years is processing of orders and tracking. In the early days, information was keypunched onto cards. This unidentified operator is busy at work at cumbersome and unforgiving equipment.

AN EARLY COMPUTER USER. The Swiss Colony was using computer technology as early as 1956. This photograph of Ethel Kubly was featured in a 1958 issue of *Electrified Industry* magazine. She is using an order scanner, which took information from the punched cards described in the top photograph to create mailing lists, shipping orders, invoices, and mailing labels.

STATE-OF-THE-ART, THEN. Tape-driven computer systems had come upon the scene by the 1960s. Here Lynda Mauermann and Willie Berndt are using a new system in 1967. The SC Data Center, incorporated in 1969, was created to offer services to affiliated companies and other businesses within a 150-mile radius.

COMMAND CENTER. Today's modern computer room command center keeps the very heart of the data center tuned and operational. From rear to front are Gary Larson, Cheryl Blosch, and Tammy Small at operations central.

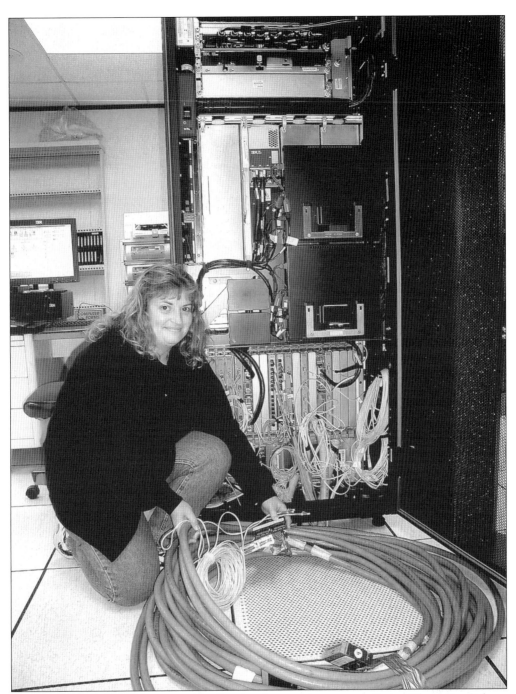

CONSTANT UPGRADES. Innovation and technology are in constant flux at The Swiss Colony. Kneeling by one of the computer mainframe panels is Cheryl Blosch. She is showing the difference between heavy cables that were once used in data center operations compared to the tiny fiber-optic cables that are now in use.

ALL AUTOMATED. Randy Iverson peeks through a virtual tape server that is a component of the SC Data Center's computer mainframe. The tapes store the customer database. A robotic arm pulls the tapes for customer order processing. Compare this to the huge racks of tapes it replaced (below), which were commonplace in older computer configurations at The Swiss Colony.

DISK STORAGE DEVICE. This unit was new in 2001. The amount of data on it at that time was equal to the data on a million high-density floppy disks. A million floppy disks would cover a football field—twice. Dennis Bliss is manager of the technical services area.

COMMUNICATIONS. Keeping various satellite locations and home order takers connected to the mainframe computer is critical. Gary Larson checks the status of communication lines in 2001. Keeping these "on-line" systems operational is a huge task.

ENGINEER AT WORK. Al Farrar, fulfillment center engineer, works on a piece of equipment in the Monroe facility. Farrar helped to perfect the company's warehouse master system. Engineers like Farrar conduct production efficiency studies, equipment upgrades, and the like. Putting technology to work to meet the needs of today's demanding customers is an important thrust in Swiss Colony operations.

The Swiss Colony®

CHOOSE 'N CHARGE®

BUY NOW
AND PAY LATER

See back of the center order form for details.

CHOOSE 'N CHARGE. This trademarked company credit offering was introduced in 1969. When The Swiss Colony began offering its own in-house credit, only Montgomery Ward, JCPenney, and Sears and Roebuck were doing so. This forerunner credit plan was quite convenient for company customers and resulted in a spurt of growth, as other competing mail-order houses had not yet begun to offer credit. The plan is used by a growing number of customers annually.

THOROUGH TRAINING. High-tech training facilities are offered by The Swiss Colony and its affiliates. From left to right are Randy Iverson, Linda Hartwig, Angie Beutler, Todd Handel, Jim Helms, and Brett Lanphier in a training session. Hartwig and Lanphier are from PDS Company; others are all employees. In training areas such as this, employees receive training in job and supervisory skills, communication skills, interpersonal skills, and safety procedures. Attending the University of Swiss Colony, employees can even earn internal degrees in various areas.

VISUAL COMMUNICATIONS. Video conferencing is used extensively. With locations in 11 communities outside its home Monroe base, this form of interaction is a step above teleconferencing, allowing more extensive and thorough business conferences. From left to right, Tami Wedig, Marc Klein, and Ann Hunter hold a session with employees at another location in Hannibal, Missouri. The Swiss Colony and its affiliates have facilities in Monroe, Madison, Dickeyville, Kenosha, and Janesville, Wisconsin; Savanna and Rockford, Illinois; DeWitt, Clinton, Peosta, and Davenport, Iowa; and Hannibal, Missouri.

SANTA'S ELVES. The Monroe fulfillment center is an unbelievable maze of conveyors, overhead moving belts, and hundreds of "elves" assembling orders for customers. Some 1,200 temporary employees at this facility alone assist the full-time staff in organized chaos. The company even

sends buses out in a 60-mile radius to neighboring cities to pick up employees and bring them to work every day during the holiday rush season.

WEB SITES MULTIPLY. The Internet has become an important marketing tool for The Swiss Colony and its affiliated companies. Since its first Web site was developed in 1997, use of the Web has grown dramatically. The first season, Internet sales were .01 percent of total sales for that catalog. Now the Internet accounts for 20 to 25 percent of the companies' total sales. This is the home page of The Swiss Colony Web site.

INTERNET GURUS. Some Internet Department employees of the marketing affiliate, incorporated in 1996, include, from left to right, Kaci Nall, Betsy Lauer, Ryan Ackerman, and Hans Bernet. The development of the Web sites has been guided by Bernet since their inception. Each of the seven affiliated catalog companies now has its own Web site.

IT ALL CULMINATES IN THIS. For a happy, satisfied customer of Swiss Colony products, the corporate mission statement sums it up: "We Deliver the Magic of Christmas Year Round. It's the pride we take, the mood we set, the anticipation we create, the satisfaction we deliver, and the memories we've etched forever in the customers' minds."

We Deliver the Magic of Christmas Year 'Round

The Swiss Colony flag flies proudly with the American flag.